PRISONER OF WAR NUMBER 2378

PRISONER OF WAR NUMBER

The True Story of a British Airman in WWII Singapore

To: Carnee

Kenneth E. Stroud

Adrian Stroud

TATE PUBLISHING
AND ENTERPRISES, LLC

Published by Tate Publishing & Enterprises, LLC
127 E. Trade Center Terrace | Mustang, Oklahoma 73064 USA
1.888.361.9473 | www.tatepublishing.com

Tate Publishing is committed to excellence in the publishing industry. The company reflects the philosophy established by the founders, based on Psalm 68:11,
"The Lord gave the word and great was the company of those who published it."

Book design copyright © 2013 by Tate Publishing, LLC. All rights reserved.
Cover design by Junriel Boquecosa
Interior design by Caypeeline Casas

Published in the United States of America

ISBN: 978-1-62746-752-0
1. Biography & Autobiography / Military
2. History / Military / World War II
13.07.11

This book is dedicated to the thousands who did not return.

ACKNOWLEDGMENTS

I wish to thank first and foremost my father, Kenneth E. Stroud, for the tremendous sacrifice he made in serving his beloved England in World War II. For this, he suffered for three and a half years. I would like to thank my wife, Laura Stroud, who encouraged me many years ago to write a book about my father's war experiences. I also wish to thank my old friend Lieutenant John McAllister of the Ridgefield Police Department, my brother-in-arms, who encouraged me for ten years to tell my dad's story. Thanks also to my old friend Officer A. Peter Biagiotti, of the Westport Police Department, for his insightful foreword. I would like to thank Karen A. Fildes and all the students from Bethel High School who worked on the Veteran's History Project. Thank you to Dean Scoville of *Police Magazine*. Thank you to Michael Dooling of the Waterbury Republican American. Thank you to my cousin Mary Portilla Stroud. I would like to thank the staff at Tate Publishing Company for the opportunity to tell my dad's story to the world. I am very grateful.

FOREWORD

Many biographies have been written about the personal heroic exploits of the men and women who served during World War II, both fact and fiction. Author Adrian Stroud, however, has been able to record for history incredible details about his father's final days as a Japanese prisoner of war. The author expertly recounts how his father and other prisoners of war displayed exceptional sacrifice, love for country, and love for one another. Royal Air Force (R.A.F.) Leading Aircraftsman, Kenneth E. Stroud's heart-wrenching daily account of his final days as a prisoner of war is a tribute to those who sacrificed so much for their country. His book is a tribute to the incredible sacrifices made by prisoners taken by the Japanese Army during the invasion of Singapore. Few men have served their country with greater devotion and dedication, or in a more professional manner.

This book is as much a memoir as a biography, as it rests largely on a long series of interviews with Mr. Kenneth E. Stroud and the personal diary he kept during his days in captivity. His detailed account takes you from his early days as a young twenty-year-old joining the Royal Air Force to his day-by-day life as Japanese prisoner of war. From boarding a ship in England in May 1940, steaming toward North Africa, and finally arriving in Singapore. His captivating account of living the "high-life" in downtown Singapore to the Japanese air attacks prior to the invasion and finally his being taken a prisoner of war.

Mr. Kenneth E. Stroud's account is not only of his personal pain and suffering, but also of those imprisoned with him. From becoming Japanese prisoner of war number *2378* to the brutal treatment of prisoners by guards as they were marched from prison camp to prison camp. The train he and other prisoners of war captors were riding being ambushed by Japanese soldiers. How he switched positions with a prisoner for "evening air" while being transported in a rail boxcar and how that same prisoner was shot between the eyes during an ambush. The deplorable living conditions in the Japanese prisoner of war camps and lack of edible food given to prisoners.

Through all these horrific events, Japanese prisoner of war # 2378, Royal Air Force (R.A.F.) Leading Aircraftsman, Kenneth E. Stroud kept a secret daily diary. Though painful for him to relive and discuss the past, it is his hope the sacrifices of those prisoners not be forgotten and that we learn from the past.

Aldo P. Biagiotti
Lieutenant Colonel (Retired)
U.S. Army
Former Instructor–United States
Military Academy WestPoint

INTRODUCTION

On February 15, 1942, British forces in Singapore surrendered to the Japanese forces. The so-called fortress had fallen. It was the largest single surrender of British forces in the country's history. It also meant a death sentence to those soldiers who would die a later, miserable death in the many Japanese prison camps in and around Singapore. For one man, Leading Aircraftsman Kenneth E. Stroud RAF service number 1196726, it was the beginning of a nightmare that would last three and a half years and remain forever burned into his memory and his very soul. He is my father, and this is the story of his days as a POW of the Japanese. I have written this book by drawing upon my father's extensive memory. The last section is his own diary entries, just as they appear in the diary he kept in the final days of the war. He witnessed history unfold and the beginning of a new life.

It is the winter of 2011. I look out the window at the Litchfield Hills of Western Connecticut. It seems a million miles and a lifetime away, from the Singapore of 1942. I return to the task of typing out my father's World War II diary. As I read the entries in it, it is hard not to get angry at the Japanese soldiers for the way they treated him. As a retired police officer, I feel my emotions rise at a great sense of injustice and at the thought of monsters that went unpunished. Brutal men operated with impunity and made thousands of other men and women suffer. I read further and choke back angry tears. I am incensed, but I must finish this. It is important that my father's story be told. Many never returned to tell their stories. Many more took their stories to the grave. When I was a boy in the 1960s, I remember playing at a neighbor's house on a summer Sunday afternoon. The boy's father came outside and yelled at us to be quiet. He worked a night job and slept during the day. I walked home and spoke to my dad, who was relaxing, reading the newspaper in the dining room. I said, "The man up the road yelled at us to be quiet!" My dad put the paper down and gazed at me. He replied quietly, "That man went ashore at D-day. You let him enjoy his peace and quiet." I never forgot that. The very thought of such incidents during that war shook me to my core. I had nothing but respect for such men. I was grateful for their bravery.

I awoke with a start one night. My father was down the hall in his bedroom. He was thrashing in his sleep and calling out. This terrified me. In the morning, I asked my mother why he had done that. She told me, "It's because of the war." I later asked my dad what scared him enough to make him scream in his sleep. He replied, "I always dream that I got out of the prison camp but was foolish enough to get captured and put back in there!" For many years, my mother forbade my father from speaking about the war. She had lived in England and had suffered through the bombings. Once, as a telephone operator, she had a bomb crash through the ceiling of the exchange and land, undetonated, on the floor near her. She picked it up and deposited it into a fire bucket of sand!

Mom told me once that she had walked down to the waterfront in her city of Weymouth, England. She witnessed the American first division soldiers entering their boats to head out to the D-day invasion. The invasion was delayed, and the soldiers became seasick but eventually shoved off for Normandy. Whenever my dad began talking about prisoner of war life, she stopped him. My mom died in 2004.

In February 2011, at the urging of my police lieutenant friend John McAllister, I contacted Karen A. Fildes. Karen is a teacher at Bethel High School in Bethel, Connecticut. Karen, and several students spent many hours interviewing my dad for a project to preserve the experiences of World War II veterans. The students were very caring and respectful. They patiently recorded three hours of video of my dad.

During a follow-up visit to my dad's house in Southbury, Connecticut, Karen was looking through a Tupperware container of dad's memorabilia from WWII. She was impressed and said to my dad, "I wish you kept a diary during your prisoner of war captivity." My dad replied, "I did," and he immediately produced a small brown notebook from the container. I was amazed. I never knew he kept a diary during the war. He told us that if the guards had found it, they would have killed him.

THE BEGINNING

The war had been raging for over a year. Dad had even stood at the gate to his home one day as a long column of British soldiers filed down his lane. The men, bedraggled and disheveled, had just been successfully evacuated by sea from the Battle of Dunkirk. They had left everything behind them on the beach, including their weapons, and gotten into anything that floated to escape the German Army. Dad was amazed to see that one soldier carried only a guitar. As a British plane flew over, Dad suddenly realized he was the only one still standing in the road. The entire troop column had dived into ditches, fearing the plane was an enemy.

On another occasion, my dad was near a railway station outside of his town of Weymouth, England. He was doing a job in telephone repair for the post office. He looked up and saw an RAF fighter plane and a Luftwaffe fighter engaged in a fierce dogfight. The German plane lost and was shot down. Dad observed the plane crash and explode in a nearby field. He quickly ran across the train tracks and through the adjacent field. The plane's wreckage was strewn across a large area. The pilot had been smashed to pieces and parts of him lay about. My dad grabbed a small souvenir of the wreckage and left before the authorities arrived. Such was life in wartime England.

My father, Kenneth Edward Stroud, joined the Royal Air Force near London in 1940. He was twenty years old. He is the son of Thomas Stroud, a Hertfordshire County Police Officer, and Frances Stroud, a homemaker. Thomas had seen action in major battles in WWI in the MMP (Military Mounted Police). Kenneth had one sibling, Reginald T. Stroud. Reg would experience much brutal combat in Burma in the British Army. He did his initial training called *square-bashing* back then on the beach at Morecambe, England. He was then transported to another RAF base: Yatesbury. Yatesbury is close to Avebury, a similar *henge* to Stonehenge.

One night, a corporal came into his barracks. My dad recognized him as a fellow engineer from the British Post Office Engineering Department in Dorchester, Dorset. He took my dad across the base to a restricted area. They walked through a gate and down a long path. This area had been designated as a center for instruction and training in *Radio Direction Finding* (RDF) and would later become universally known as RADAR. Dad found out later that that corporal managed to keep himself in England all through the war. Dad began his radar training in earnest. One night, while studying the screen, he saw a very large group of enemy planes inbound to bomb a city. He later learned they had observed German planes bombing Coventry in one of the most devastating air raids of the war.

Dad then boarded a ship at Birkenhead starting a voyage to he knew not where in May of 1940. The ship went north toward Iceland and curved south along Canada, then past South America, and then finally, east toward Africa. His ship was in a convoy of troop ships escorted by Royal Navy destroyers. The route was deliberate to avoid U-boats that were constantly hunting for the convoys to torpedo them. One night near Freetown, Africa, his ship was bumped by a cruiser causing some damage. The ship stayed one night in Freetown for repairs. The next day, the convoy came south around the Cape of Good Hope, and then it turned north. At one point, a ship containing female nurses passed near them and the men waved. All contact between ships was via semaphore. One morning, round about May 27, Dad awoke and saw that their destroyer escorts were all gone. The men were frightened. They later learned that the destroyers had had to leave to attack and help sink the German battleship, *Bismarck*.

From Freetown, the convoy continued on a Southerly way, around the Cape of Good Hope, and headed north.

The ship temporarily stopped at Durban, and my dad was transferred to a parked cruiser, which immediately got under way. It was scary because the ship had no escort. While on the cruiser one night, Dad spent his twenty-first birthday on sentry duty on deck. This while officers nearby mingled with female nurses. He then arrived in Singapore. He was then stationed at a Royal Australian Air Force base: Sembawang. He slept under mosquito nets due to terrible biting by mosquitoes. This became their base to live at. The RAF then took possession of the Cathay Building in downtown Singapore, which was a skyscraper. My dad and the other radar airmen set up their radar antennas on the roof of the building for detecting of expected Japanese air attacks. The men occupied four luxury suites that they had commandeered in the penthouse. The technical RDF equipment was set up here. The downstairs of the building was a movie theatre. It was closed, and the RAF took the A/C equipment for its own use. Dad had many adventures with the Australian soldiers in the area. Life was great in Singapore. People lived well. Australian women ran many cafes in town, like the coffee shop where Dad frequented.

One day, Dad was in downtown Singapore. He ran into a group of sailors from the HMS *Repulse*. Dad befriended the newcomers and showed them around town. He took them to the coffee shop. The next day, Dad got news at his base that the *Repulse* had been sunk that day by Japanese warships. The very men dad had spent time with were all dead.

Dad became friends with an officer, Flight Lt. Sydney E. Catt. Catt was a fascinating man who was signals officer at Seletar Air Base. Syd had possession of top secret cipher books at the base. Dad once dined at Lieutenant Catt's home and played the piano for Catt and his wife. Catt's children were asleep upstairs. Syd had a beautiful home and was very kind to my father. I cannot overstate what a marvelous man Syd was. He helped many people in the Singapore area as the end neared. Many of the officers had beautiful homes in Singapore. Life in Singapore was carefree, and the war was a million miles away and would never touch my dad and his mates, or so they thought!

One day, Dad was on the roof of the Cathay building. He met the Singapore Chief of Police, Chief Superintendant Camp. Dad and he got to talking, and Dad discovered that Camp's father had been a policeman with Dad's father in Hertfordshire, and the Camp family had lived next door to my dad! Camp related to dad that the Japanese had spies in Singapore that would disappear down an understreet tunnel when Camp's men went to round them up.

Some days later, air attacks started. The planes that the British had in Singapore were left over, antiquated WWI biplanes—useless against the new Zeroes. The British planes only topped out at about 300 mph. My dad and the other airmen had no weapons and very rudimentary training with them anyway. One morning, the powers that be gave orders to my dad to get his RAF kit and leave in thirty minutes. His name had been drawn from a hat, and he had a place on a truck. Other men had no place on the truck and had to stay. They may have escaped and been better off than my dad. Only history knows. He was to evacuate because Japanese forces were heading into Singapore. He and the men went down the rear side of the Cathay building and the group got in a group of luxury cars at the curb, which had been commandeered from a group of millionaires.

While en route to the docks, they drove through downed power and telephone lines. These were hanging in ribbons. At one point, a British *red cap*, or a military policeman, flagged them down. The men picked him up and drove him to the docks with them. These air attacks were apparently a prelude to the main invasion. At the docks, they saw women and children being loaded onto a ship. Dad and the men were put on a flat-bottomed boat that had been used for hunting river pirates. They slept on deck since night had fallen. They had to wait for daylight to leave because the buoys in the harbor were mined. Safe navigation had to be done in daylight.

The men then sailed to Batavia through the Sunda Strait. They disembarked the boat and slept in an old disused Dutch high school. The radar equipment they had anxiously awaited delivery of came from the Mid East. The men reluctantly smashed it with axes to avoid its use by the Japanese. My dad was there at this area for days. He went shopping. He saw how the Dutch lived in splendor in homes in the area. Next, the men were told things were "going sour" and they were placed on American trucks. They traveled east through Java to a port town on the south coast; Tjilatjap.

Once the men arrived at Tjilatjap, they waited to see what the RAF would do with them. My dad thought they would all get off via submarines surfaced off the coast. He saw enemy planes looking for targets. The planes were part of a Japanese invasion only days away. Dusk came and the men were put into a warehouse. The next day, they were put on trucks and driven to a train. The RAF and RAAF airmen were loaded onto the train in stuffy metal cattle cars. The sides of the cattle cars had an entry aperture and air passed into the cars via this opening.

The conditions were inhuman as the men traveled on the train in the moonlight. The airmen sat on the car's floor in rows. My dad longed to sit on the edge and dangle his feet out the aperture to get air. He argued with the man on his right to do this. The man, winning the argument, sat dangling his feet out. Suddenly, the air was full of bullets flying through the car. A Japanese ambush team, probably in the trees, opened up on the unarmed RAF and RAAF personnel stuffed like cattle in the train cars. The man who enjoyed my dad's evening air was drilled right between the eyes, killed instantly where he sat. My dad, his left knee up against the next man's right knee, saw that man's knee cap severely injured, leaving my dad unscathed. Mayhem reigned as the trains was raked with machine gun and mortar fire. The Javanese train drivers leapt off the engine and ran into the jungle. The engine boiler, riddled by bullets, miraculously had enough steam in it to allow the train to continue out of the kill zone. Many casualties had been sustained.

Once the train came to a halt, the men disembarked. They marched through the night until they came upon a hut on the side of the tracks. Here, the wounded were left in hopes that the Japanese advancing forces would care for them. Later in the war, my father spoke with a man who had been left wounded in the hut. He witnessed Japanese soldiers bayoneting and shooting the wounded. He faked being dead as he lay in a pile of corpses. He was able to jump out a window and flee. Presently, the man was picked up by Japanese officers traveling in a car. They, unlike the cretins who had slaughtered the unarmed wounded in the hut, appeared cultured. They were quite decent to the airman and they dropped him at a POW camp.

Meanwhile, Dad and the others came upon a bridge that had been blown up over a river. They learned that two trains had been traveling with airmen aboard. One had been ambushed earlier than dad's train, and it was now derailed. My dad was on the second train. As the trains' passengers, unarmed airmen, left the train, they marched over a large suspension bridge spanning a river near Maos. Dutch forces, seeing the approaching men, blew up the bridge near midnight. Many casualties were sustained and injured men fell into the river only to be met by crocodiles. The middle spans of the bridge collapsed. The men, including my dad, had to jump across the sections to reach the other side. He had the presence of mind, before entering the water, to take off his shoes and tie the laces together. He then draped the shoes around his neck to keep them dry. This was now about 2:00 a.m.

Upon reaching the other side of the river, my dad and the men encountered a Dutch officer. He was distraught. He told them he thought the approaching men were Japanese, and he blew the bridge. He was horrified to learn the men were *Allies*! The men slept in a field that night. Dad tried to settle down. He took out his issue raincoat. He had folded it up and used it as a pillow on the train earlier. Now, as he unfolded it, he saw a series of holes appear in it. Not only had Dad cheated death twice on the train, but this was evidence of a third time. Bullets had passed though the raincoat that he had been resting his head on. Hours later, he would board yet another train that then deposited the men at a station. The airmen were then put in a barn near an airport. Dad could see crashed British WWI era planes on the field. He cut a leather fuel bladder off of one and sewed it in to a pouch to keep him busy.

Dad in training in the R.A.F. Dad is in the center.

The Cathay Building showing the RADAR antennas.

Dad on the roof of the Cathay Building showing RADAR antennas.

Dad sitting on the roof of the Cathay Building before 1942.

Dad in Singapore 1942.

Singapore 1942 street scene.

Singapore 1942 boat in the harbor.

Dad's P.O.W. tag.

FROM · Mrs. F. E. STROUD
SARNIA. ICEN LANE.
BROADWEY. WEYMOUTH
Feb 4th 1944 · DORSET. ENG.

DEAREST BELOVED KEN
ARE YOU STILL ALRIGHT
ALL LONGING TO SEE YOU.
ROLL ON WHEN WE MEET.
COURAGE DARLING.
  GOD BLESS YOU LOVINGLY MUM.

FROM. MRS. F. E. STROUD
SARNIA. ICEN LANE.
BROADWEY. WEYMOUTH
DORSET· ENG.   2/....4 .

DEAREST BELOVED KEN
HAVE YOU HEARD FROM US YET?.
YOURS RECEIVED
STILL THINKING OF YOU
LOVE FROM EVERYONE
GOD BLESS YOU DEAR. HOPE ON.
  LOVING MUM.

Dad's WWII postcards

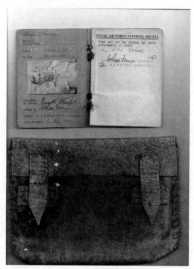

Dads R.A.F. ID and a pouch he made from a crashed planes fuel tank.

Japanese $10 bill signed by Lord Louis Mountbatten and his wife.

Dad returning home stepping off the HMS Alamazora.
Dad is in the very center, on the gangplank.

BUCKINGHAM PALACE

The Queen and I bid you a very warm welcome home.

Through all the great trials and sufferings which you have undergone at the hands of the Japanese, you and your comrades have been constantly in our thoughts. We know from the accounts we have already received how heavy those sufferings have been.   We know also that these have been endured by you with the highest courage.

We mourn with you the deaths of so many of your gallant comrades.

With all our hearts, we hope that your return from captivity will bring you and your families a full measure of happiness, which you may long enjoy together.

George R.I.

September 1945.

King George IV letter to returing P.O.W.s.

Reginald T. Stroud (l) and Kenneth E. Stroud (r)

Mom & Dad wedding

Dad & Mom on their honeymoon on the Isle of Jersey

My father Kenneth E. Stroud, age 92. This picture was taken of him near his home in Connecticut in May 2013. My father is very grateful to have lived such a long life. As my dad always says, "God has given me a wonderful life to make up for the many years of misery that I suffered."

PRISONERS OF WAR

In the morning, Japanese soldiers arrived. The airmen were lined up and marched to the far side of the airport. As they marched, Japanese planes flew overhead. My dad had a sick feeling that at any moment they would be strafed and killed where they stood. They were not. The men then set up beds in nearby hangars. The Japanese taught them simple phrases to use in Japanese. They would utter one phrase when requesting a bathroom break, *Benjo e ikimasu*, and another phrase to return, *Benjo e ikimasen*. They were also taught to number off in Japanese when in formation—*ichi* for 1, *ni* for 2, *san* for 3, etc. The Japs insisted that the prisoners bow to them when they approached. The nearest man would call the other prisoners to attention. If any man failed to bow to a guard, he would be beaten. The men feared the *kempeita* the most. They were the Japanese Military Secret Police. Dad was issued a small, gray metal tag with a safety pin attached. On the tag was dad's prisoner of war prisoner number in English and in Japanese. Dad became prisoner number *2378* for the next three and a half years.

The men slept there tightly guarded. Many incidents took place. The British pulled fast ones on the Japs as often as they could. It was a them-versus-us scenario. They were there for some days, perhaps even months. Dad even remembered marching down a road one day, and a group of German soldiers marched past them. The Germans were quite cheerful and waved. The war was over for them. They were now interned by their former Allies, the Japanese.

The men were then traveled to Surabaya. They were placed in a camp called Jaarmarkt in Dutch or yearly market in English. This was an empty place with bamboo hut accommodations. The men felt that the Japs were trying to figure out what to do with them and seemed ill-equipped for the task. The men were immediately told by the Japanese commander that his country never signed the Geneva Convention treatises, and therefore, the Japanese would not honor it. It was made apparent to them that the Japs considered the British less than human because they had allowed themselves to be taken prisoner. They should have all killed themselves instead! My father was placed in this camp with seventy civilian Dutch doctors and business leaders, all male. This was strictly forbidden by the Convention, now a mute point. The doctors had only their minds; they had no instruments and no medications to treat the sick. The Japs took all the males out of the city of Surabaya, leaving the women and children. On one occasion, the Japs allowed the women to visit their husbands in a field, which was part of the camp. Every day, something was happening. Hundreds of people living and dying. Some officers were segregated from the enlisted men.

Amazingly, Dad met his old friend Lt. Syd Catt at this camp. Catt's journey had paralleled dads as both men tried to escape capture when the Japs first invaded Singapore. During formation one day, Catt was marched out of the camp, with a group of other officers, by Jap guards. Dad assumed he had been tortured or executed. He knew that when men were marched out by the Japs, they didn't return. The days stretched into months. Dad lived day to day until a year or two had passed.

One day, Dad was in agony with a tooth problem, and guards marched him from the Jaarmarkt to a nearby high school camp which had a dentist. While marching there, he was forced to slog through deep mud. His left big toe struck an unseen tree root, which immediately pulled the nail up. His toe would remain damaged by this for the rest of his life. The dentist, having only one crude tool, pulled his bad tooth, sans anesthetic, of course. Another doctor came in and treated the toe.

Not all the guards were cruel, but most were. The camp consisted of British, Dutch, and native peoples. Civilians, mostly businessmen, and military men were mixed. Few in number were American GIs. Dad did meet some Americans in the camp who seemed to be mostly Mexican Americans from Texas. One American soldier would often shave his head into a Mohawk which fascinated everybody. Dad had never really seen many Yanks.

Some months later, my dad and the other men were ordered to leave the Jaarmarkt Camp. They were taken to the docks and placed into the hold of the ship, at Surabaya. The walk down into the hold was absolutely awful. Men were crammed into every ounce of space. The conditions on the ship were inhuman, appalling. There was a lack of proper ventilation, sanitation, food, and water. One man immediately became sick and was roughly taken off the ship and subsequently died. The hellish voyage began my dad's journey into an even more nightmarish life ahead, across the islands. The ship continued its way south past the Spice Islands—Bali, Lombok, Sumba, and Sumbawa, continuing past the Flores Group. The ship then headed north to Ambon and its final destination, the island of Haruku, and a yet-to-be-built prison camp. A landing strip was also planned.

At the new camp, it was made painfully clear that escape, or an unwillingness to do what the Japs told them to do, would be met with a bullet. The commandant told the men that this island was called Haruku, and it was patrolled. The water around the island had sharks in it and patrolling Japanese boats. Dad surmised that the Japanese were using the chain of islands on a step-by-step basis, to attack and conquer Australia. This was their plan—invasion. The composition of the island was coral. The prisoners were used to create runways, out of the coral, for the invasion of Australia. The final punch out would be from Haruku to Australia. He heard sometime later that the Japs actually did attack one Australian city, Darwin.

The work was brutal in the never-ending hot sun, with little water and even less food. Whenever he could, Dad and the other men would loaf off and stop working. They certainly had no intention of finishing the runways, so the Japs could bomb their fellow British in Australia. This had to be done with great caution, however, for the guards would quickly and severely punish loafers. The men would dream constantly of food. This feeling would take over their thoughts to the exclusion of all else, even booze, women, or cigarettes. Men died and the other men buried them. A large burial ground was next to the camp. The men told each other to fight and stay alive! These men were my dad's buddies. Some men, who were desperately ill, would simply lie on their sleeping positions and give up. Dad and his mates would bury them the next day.

The men would walk down to an eating area. The cooking was done in great big barrels, using water from the nearby stream. Certain men, with a background in cooking, took care of that chore. Men came down with both *wet* and *dry* beriberi, from malnutrition, and many other diseases. The men would suffer with diarrhea or dysentery. My dad once saw a man's scrotum enlarge like a bowling ball bag from the dry form. Anything that swelled and filled with fluid could only be lanced to treat it. My dad suffered from the dry form, and his legs were constantly swelling. The water would back up the legs to a terrific size. You could push down with your thumb, and a minute later, the depression would come back up.

Their diet consisted of a type of dirty rice and whatever they could find to eat. The Dutch in the camp told Dad that this rice was the garbage that would normally only be used as a crop fertilizer. The quality of the rice was that poor. The guards were Japanese soldiers and some Koreans, whom the Japs had impressed into service. They were equally cruel to the prisoners, although the Koreans more so at times. One guard, which the men called the rat, was particularly sadistic. He had spent some time in California before the war and could speak some crude English. He was a translator who at times would mistranslate what the prisoners would say to the guards. This would result in the prisoner being bashed. The men used to wonder if this was deliberate.

After a long period, Dad and a group of the men were put on a ship which sailed from Haruku, in a westerly direction. They surmised when they passed the southern tip of the Celebes, that they were headed back to Surabaya. The ship put into Surabaya, and the men had to slide a distance down the side of the ship, to the dockside. The men were so weak they risked injury in the movement. Dad was amazed he didn't break his legs. They were then packed on a train headed to Batavia. The group was then placed in a camp located at a disused barracks. Toilets were a hole in a concrete floor, over which you squatted.

A group of Japanese and Australian doctors examined the prisoners. A Jap doctor pushed in on my dad's side, on his spleen, which caused him considerable pain. He did this to many POWs. Later, an Australian doctor told Dad that he thought the Japs weren't even doctors and that maybe they extracted pleasure from abusing the prisoners. It appeared that the Japs were looking for the fittest men. Dad was suspicious and thought the Japs may have been gathering men for work in Japan. He had a bad feeling about this, and at formation, he faked a knee injury. The guards passed him over and put the other men on a ship. Dad found out later that this ship had been sunk by Allied ships. During this entire time period, Dad's mother, Frances Stroud, had been mailing post cards to him via the Red Cross. The Japanese received the cards and hoarded them, never telling the prisoners of their existence. The cards held heartrending messages of hope and love for dad, and high hopes that he was alive and well. The letters she sent to my dad were returned marked No Trace. The Air Ministry told her that my dad had to be regarded as missing.

By this time, the US forces had begun to close in on the Japs via the Philippines. My dad was eventually put on another ship, from Batavia, to some unknown destination! He ended up back in Singapore, where the nightmare had all begun. This is where the invasion of Singapore had started. Dad was placed in the River Valley Camp. Here, amongst the other military prisoners, he met survivors of the bridge on the River Kwai. These men were British Army. Dad and his group were Royal Air Force. The army group had long hair, and dad's group had short hair due to differing military grooming and health standards. Dad's RAF group kiddingly called the other group the long hairs.

One day, a Dutch interpreter came to see my dad and the others. He asked for anyone with a technical background to accompany him. My dad followed him into an office. There, he saw a beautifully made radio set. The interpreter told him the Japs could not get the thing to work. Apparently, it was vitally important that the Japanese soldiers hear something on the radio. Heretofore, if the POWs were ever caught with a radio set, they would be immediately executed. Dad began adjusting the set. He discovered there was nothing wrong with the set. He turned the volume up to make his adjustments. Whenever he did this, a guard would immediately turn the volume down. Frustrated, Dad told the interpreter, "How am I expected to fix this if this idiot won't let me hear it?" The Dutch interpreter passed this on and the guard, nodding, strode off. Dad turned the volume up and what he heard shocked him. The Americans had dropped some kind of special bomb on Japan. The end was near! Upon returning to the other prisoners, he passed the hopeful news to them.

Eventually, my dad was moved from this camp, in the hills, to a temporary prison camp near the docks at Singapore. These were the final days. My dad obtained a notebook from a Dutch POW in that camp. He felt that when he could, he would take notes on his final days in the camp. The journal entries that follow are written in his own words.

K. E. Stroud
1196726

Juniata Notes

Diary
From date of Jap. surrender

Home Address
"Sarnia",
Icen Lane,
Broadwey,
Weymouth,
Dorset

Property of Kenneth E. Stroud
1196726 RAF

August 17, 1945, Friday

Went to work in hills on heavy log carrying up slippery muddy slopes behind Gillman Barracks. A most miserable rainy day, set in decrepit Chinese dwelling hovel next to Nip. Store, schrammed with cold, covered with sack in lieu of shirt. Work started on urgent job to be done at once, extra rice promised us. Enough said, starving hungry, plunged into work but to our amazement 3.0 p m Japs recalled all the little parties of 7 men working in brush. Returned straight to Morse Rd., Camp, found all parties including Pulu Brani returned, bringing news of Lanjong Pagar and Pasir Panjang having also been recalled. Wild rumours of End of War.

August 18, 1945, Saturday

Work or not? Everyone worked up. Officer says last working party day of war, interpreter says end of war, still dubious. Working parties parade but cancelled; great joy at "yasmi"* day, (* actually YASUME "rest") all excited. 9.0 p m rumours of move, 11 p m "lights out" moving in morning.

August 19, 1945, Sunday

Pasir Panjang chaps who changed camps with us returned to Morse Rd. while we were sitting on kit, waiting to leave. & the remainder passed our camp on their way back to Tanjong Pagar. "Jerries" with full kit passed gate on lorries, waving & laughing like madmen. We returned on lorries to Tanjong Pagar Camp natives waving & V—signing us, Akimoto bowing & smiling greeted us, small drafts coming into camp from all over the place such as Pulu Damar War definitely over.

August 20, 1945, Monday

British Navy expected, somewhat prematurely I think people staying up all night in bright moonlight, speaking to Chinese over fence (sign of the times) Went to bed feeling ill overwrought with excitement. Wt. 7st. 8lb.

August 21, 1945, Tuesday

Farce continues, ½ free ½ P.O.W. We ignore Nips now, fires started on camp. Canadian Red Cross parcels (1 each) with clothing, socks & pants issued.

August 22, 1945, Wednesday

Heard war was over on 16th but nothing official, told that Singapore didn't give in until 2 days later. More issues including battledress.

August 23, 1945, Thursday

Singlet, shorts, socks, face towel issued, socks English, no sign of our people yet.

August 24, 1945, Friday

Still enjoying parcel. Some stomach trouble, enteritis. Started embroidering props. & eagles; still more clothing. Indians came into camp last night from drome—building party in Johore jungle at Kulai leaving drome unfinished. Formerly 4/22nd Mountain Batt., previously manned 6" Naval guns Seletas Naval Base defense. Boots issued, none myself, big feet!

August 25, 1945, Saturday

4 months to Xmas Day. 1st B-S parade in battledress & new clothes very smart, "Hotfers" eyes popping out of heads. Separate English cookhouse now.

August 26, 1945, Sunday

Decree from Gen. Sito on behalf Allied generals at Rangoon. No escaping, full Brit. Discipline, & mail may be dropped on camps by ' chute in next few days. 1/3 lb fresh Aussie butter & tin cheese (1 each) issued; rumors of more tomorrow Indian soldier of cerebral malaria & enteritis, such hard lives. 1st fresh meat meal (beef) ever received in Sing. From Japs since leaving Makasura (Batavia) camp.

Beef stew & steak pudding. 4 months to Boxing Day! Everyone saying "Shall we get home in time?" At least a kind of Boxing Day in advance.

August 27, 1945, Monday

P.R.O. 1 issued by F/O Murray Wrote topical article for Hal Levenssohn's "memories of Malaya". Considerable beri-beri on camp with enteritis as matter of course. A day very sick, tummy trouble—corn beef at night.

August 28, 1945, Tuesday

Rough agreement signed yesterday according to "gen"., but this may be untrue. During issue of tiffin 1st Allied kite flew over, then 2 more, leaflets dropped, plane so low that "erk" was visible at trapdoor throwing them out. Bundles fell on Camp square, Chinese kids rushed in to get them; written in Chinese script & Tamil. No ordinary roundels, terrific excitement & rushing in & out with food in mouth. White dot, blue circle, no red centre, 4 engines similar to Liberator. Expected inspection by Gen. Sito, but as usual Nip. Captain arrived.

August 29, 1945, Wednesday

Wt. now 8st 4lb, 10lb 1 week! Had 2nd Red Cross parcel 1 to 3 men & lovely new books from American Red Cross more boots arrived. All these as result of visit of 3 Lt. Cols. 1 Eng. 1 Aus. 1 Dut. From Changi. Aussie addressed us saying Aussie troops expected September 1st, Col. Holmes is our CO; that he (Aussie) had honour to be 1st Brit. Officer to leave Changi on Allied business re. possible transfer of Alexandra hospital for our sick. Tells of daily drop in Nip. supremacy. Said that on entering conference room, Nip. Senior officers rose & bowed to him first & he remarked "It went down pretty good I must say!" Promised bi-weekly concert parties from Changi if here long enough.

August 30, 1945, Thursday

Managed to get pr. Of Jap. Boots at last, not a bad fit. Visit of Swiss Consul & Red Cross delegate, very affable people, they are treated now by Nips, with great deference, previously ignored in Singapore, "hands tied & allowed no connexion with P.O.W.".s. Said we may fly to Rangoon & thence straight home as many kites at Rangoon He objected to our lying on floor. Said "your bones must be very sore after 3 ½ years." Chorus of "You wouldn't think so!" Gift of 2 pigs from Chinese, pork soup at supper, embroidered 2 medical collar dogs for Sgt. Joc Till.

August 31, 1945, Friday

Ref. library opened today. Obtained fine book "A Guide to Great Orchestral Music" by Sigmund Spaeth pub. by Messrs. Random House Inc. New York calling themselves "Modern Library" More cigs. Issued. 1st bread issue 1 loaf 3"x2" for 2 men! Visit by English Paratroops dropped yesterday at Changi, of new Air Supply Corps (2 Admin. off. 2 Med. off. & 2 orderlies) Brought in medical supplies; were wearing greenish KD. With paratroop wings. Evening meal rice, pork stew, steamed pork pie & "cream doofer".

September 1, 1945, Saturday

Saw my 1st paratroop officers in camp, wearing their green & brown patchwork slip-on jacket, shirt underneath with black "pips" & yellow bar, red lion of India on each shoulder, new medal ribbons on left breast, paratroop wings on right red beret with chromium paratroop wings badge therein. Press photographer unofficially in camp, formerly of Straits Times. Taking shots of malnutrition, beri-beri & Jap. Starvation. My picture taken sitting on bed in hut. Message to us from South East Asia Command read out, some Red Cross comforts given out.

September 2, 1945, Sunday
Official End of War of Six Years

Strange, it began & ended on a Sunday. Treaty signed by Allies at 10.30 a.m. today. Some rioting outside camp firecrackers etc. Chinese Communist Party & some former I.N.A. members. Radio installed in camp, heard Waikiki, All India Radio, SEAC Station Ceylon, 25m. band & B.B.C. news. Heard Rob. Cleaver at organ. Tins of milk, cigarettes, eggs & papayas. Marmalade pud. For dinner. Incidentally large flags of CHINA flying brazenly outside; news of considerable starvation (pork at 500 Jap. $ per hatie (1 1/3 lb)). Some explosions today outside. After even parade, went to Thanksgiving service held by Dutch padre' from Changi, a very sincere man but strange form of English. Afterwards listened to B.B.C. very much pepped up now. Heard news given out; heard recording of the signing on the "Missouri", heard actual voices of Gen. MacArthur presiding, Adm. Nimitz & Pres. Truman. After this a variety called "Navy Mixture". Absolutely topholer, most enjoyable; now we know what we have been missing for 3 ½ years.

September 3, 1945, Monday

Breakfast 2 boiled eggs & 2 fried biscuits with chicken & bacon paste on top. Issues of tin pineapple (1 each) huge tins of Nestle powdered milk & papayas. 6 years ago this terrible war began, Mum and I standing by radio at 11 a.m. when Mr. Chamberlain broadcast.

September 4, 1945, Tuesday

On guard this morning RAF turn & RAF Sgt. Guard; very smart turn out considering 3 ½ years farce. 11 a m Colour Hoisting Parade! All camp present, really smart parade, Eng. Amer. & Dut. Colours hoisted, Brit. & Dut. Nat. Anthems lustily sung. Paratroop officers arrived just at moment of hoisting. Simultaneously at 11 a.m. Jap officers went on cruiser to rendezvous about 10 miles off Singapore to meet our Senior Naval Officers on H.M.S. Sussex, later in afternoon British Cruiser (Cleopatra) arrived in Keppel Harbour & 6 or 7 went round to Selitas Naval Base. 1st march organized in afternoon for exercise, proceeding to Middle Wharf & saw newly arrived cruiser. English landings expected tomorrow. Good supper for guard "vegemite" broth.

September 5, 1945, Wednesday

Very bad stomach from overeating. Unwisely went for route march on Middle Wharf at 10 a.m. Climbed up a spare gangway to see cruiser at anchor off bollyer's Quay. Just after tiffin (approx 2 pm Tokyo time) climbed tree in camp to see our good old fleet coming in "line astern", cruiser "Sussex" leading, making for Mid. Wharf. & 4 big transports. Sea was rather misty, could perceive 14 or 15 in "line astern" stretching to horizon & still coming. Indians, Sikhs & Panjaubi troops landed in afternoon also Ghurkas. I met host of Press Photographers at back of camp. Had my photo taken by at least a doz. cameras by Navy, Army & RAF correspondents. 2 of them took my name, number + address to cable home immediately. 5th Div. Indians, been in Abbysinia etc with 8th Army. Came prepared for trouble, disarmed Nip troops. Brought 2 reporters into camp, yarned to & questioned them, 1 a very nice fellow from "Sunday Standard". 6 p.m. mess parade, camp taken over by new Major of R.A. Broke out of camp in evening, down to docks. "Lords of all we surveyed" Official guests of Captain & Commander compliments of Rear Admiral Holland. Given our 1st slap-up European meal in PO's Mess (42)+ after smashing concert by ship's orchestra, one of best in fleet aboard H.M.S. Sussex the flagship, wonderful time, escorted back by Naval patrol. Lt. Com., P.M.O. of ship presided, welcome by "Jack" brought tears to our eyes to think that we belong to someone again. Stayed up half the night with M.P.'s outside camp. Fire down at docks, some queer happenings.

September 6, 1945, Thursday

Officially attached now to 23rd brigade 5th. Ind. Div., borrowed pencils off M.P.'s & wrote 2 Air Mails, one to Peggy. In afternoon went Mid. Wharf, wait to 4 pm to go aboard ship had tot of watered Jamaica Rum, very nice. 4 pm. Boarded Sussex had 5 p.m. tea, had complete tour of Radar gear on ship. Wonderful to see my old job again, grand apparatus. Also saw WT gear. Lady Louis Mountbatten expected but didn't see her. Cinema show given to all P.O.W's in godown, film "Gentleman Jim", with Errol Flynne, enjoyed it immensely, but sound boomy

September 7, 1945, Friday

Breakfast tinned bacon! Dhobied clothes & went to lunch on H.M.T. Derbyshire. Roast beef, spuds & peas with vermicelli in milk. Talked to nursing sisters most of day, 4 p.m. went on Sussex with load of bananas & papaya Had good time, Sussex entertaining Ex POW's sailors from Changi. Returned camp 11 pm. Went for walk downtown with M.P.'s had coffee at little stall in Chinese back streets.

September 8, 1945, Saturday

Wt. 8 st:6 ½ lb. Went for jaunt downtown by Collyer's Quay & High St. Bought Chinese girl's satin-silk pajama suit for Mac. of "Sussex" also watch for self & another which doesn't go. Evening on board Sussex tour round 8" guns. Mac bunked ship & came into our P.O.W. camp.

September 9, 1945, Sunday

Went downtown for watch repair spent all morning looking for another for "Sparks" In end success, had tea with Military Police in their billet & then to docks. Not allowed, but boarded Sussex for ½ hr. then to Red Cross ship with sick from Changi aboard & Krangi. Met hospital sisters & returned as guide on big "De Soto" to their hospitals Victoria & Goodwood Park Hotel. Mt. Lt. Col. O.C. Repatriation took him to conference at Goodwood & returned via Cathay & waterfront.

September 10, 1945, Monday

9 a.m. driver of "deSoto", a POW from Krangi called for me. Took RAPWI off. To all P.W. camps, Changi, Adam Rd., Sime Rd., Krangi & returned 2 pm, hungry, via-esplanade

& Collyer's Quay. D.R.O.'s state moving Wed! 4 pm down to dock to Sussex, dodging sentry After supper, film shown in shed 16 "You can't do this to me!" (Ann Southern). Back camp 11 pm Had to write official sheet of P.W. experiences

September 11, 1945, Tuesday

8 st 91/2 lb Spent nearly all day downtown with Mac. Ken & 3 other P.O.'s bargaining for silk etc. Shops which were completely empty already filled with goods & silks hidden 4 yrs from Japs. ENSA concert in camp, didn't go down to Sussex at 6.30 pm after dinner sat on "B" gun deck in cool. Lots of clothes in store ready for issue.

September 12, 1945, Wednesday

Lots of clothes issued. Singlet jersey, towel etc. Stayed in camp. Lord Louis & Lady Mountbatten visited our camp. Great day of official signing of surrender of Singapore & 1 ½ million square miles. He told us that Kempi-tai & Commandants would be treated as war criminals. Maj. Gen Sito gaoled "with his shoes off" as Louis said. Obtained both autographs on back of Jap 10 $ bill. Boarded Sussex later, saw film of Bud Abbott.

September 13, 1945, Thursday

Saw Doc, am swollen with beriberi, put on A&D (halibut oil). More clothes incl. blanket. Obtained sunglasses & case for 1 pkt of Players. Out with Mac. After lunch discovered loss of L5, asked for advance from office on my return. Later saw Major & obtained £5 more. On Sussex in evening for last dinner, saw film & talked rest of time.

September 14, 1945, Friday

Ginger Mosley got me Dutch bayonet used by Japs. Went down to Sussex for last time, nearly wet through in rain. Like losing a 2nd home. Feet badly swollen beri-beri. Aussies left camp for Changi later I went to Clifford Pier on M.L. to HMS VERUL a.m. & new "V" class destroyer. Had roast mutton, peas & "spuds", concert after. Had to pass H.M.S Nelson on way, a mighty vessel!

September 15, 1945, Saturday

Went downtown for last time, bought crocodile hide wallet & a Parker Pen for 10 rupees (15/-), good bargain. "Fall in facing the boat." At last the old saying has come true. 1 p.m. parade. Down to boat at 2 p.m. & by 4 p.m. was aboard H.M.T. "ALMANZORA" of Royal Mail Line (15000 t.) on A deck, sect. 5 (1).

September 16, 1945, Sunday

Very restful night in hammock awoke early, am mess orderly. M.O. has started us on 2/3 ration. Afternoon pulled out into "Roads" alongside "Nelson"

September 17, 1945, Monday

Still in "Roads". Some civies kicked up now, said boat wasn't good enough, were told answer & went ashore. "City of Canterbury" pulled alongside this morning—loaded with Indians; ships in convoy order. On sick parade for HAD ointment & vit. Tabs. 10.30 am boat stations 10 deck. At last at 3 p.m. the great moment, ship underway. Very heavy storm overnight had to sleep below.

September 18, 1945, Tuesday

Passed Port Swettenham early this morning, saw Doc & got 40 sulphur-grenadine tabs. Been to W.C. 20 times in 24 hrs. Good food bringing us out in all sorts of rashes.

September 19, 1945, Wednesday

Clocks retarded 1 hour. On sick parade, diarrhea stopped, put on multivit. tabs. RAF parade 11 pm; forms to fill in for relatives to meet us at dockside. Boat tossing a bit today. Wrote special Air Mail from home, don't suppose it will be posted for some days yet.

September 20, 1945, Thursday

Rather rough night but slept well. Boat tossing a lot, middle of Bay of Bengal, steward says, lots of undercurrents causing boat heaving. Ship's birthday, 30 yrs old.

September 21, 1945, Friday

Anniversary of 1st mail from home in Makasura. Finished off letters to Peggy & Mum. Received pay (£1) & posted letters. Played bridge with Matron & Padre Tucker. Matron has had 5 yrs in Ouetta during earthquake.

September 22, 1945, Saturday

Spent most of day on F deck, amongst davits. Issue of 100 cigs. & 2 boxes matches. W/C Wills-Sanford O.C. R.A.F. was also oc troops on Sibajak (41) coming out, tried to make RAF sleep in bottom hold, but after considerable trouble was over-ruled by O.C. Troops. Expect to dock tomorrow Had a look around W.T. cabin. Dour Scot. Chief W/OP. not very cordial.

September 23, 1945, Sunday

5.30 am Aldis lamp signaling daylight proved it an aircraft carrier on starboard, land also visible in distance. 10.30 am played for Church Service in 1st class lounge, Padre Goss preaching. During sermon we pulled into Colombo harbor, tooting violently on sirens, after we had passed breakwater, a wonderful reception, vociferous cheering from Naval cruiser, carrier & destroyer. RAF & RN launches alongside, Staff Officers come aboard at dinner time asking if any complaints were special SEAC medical commission due to civilian incident at Singapore. Later I chatted to Air Marshall Goddard, a very fine gentleman, Absolutely no side nowadays. Said we should have gone ashore today but coolie strike stopped scheme. 8.30 pm ENSA concert troup aboard, straight from England & Iceland. Gave grand concert & something to remember for some time to come.

September 24, 1945, Monday

9 a.m. went ashore at Colombo, returned 3.45 p.m. Marvellous reception at Echelon Bks. Ceylonese bagpipe band greeted us at "Melbourne" jetty & R.A.F. bagpipe band & R.M. band discoursed music during day. Fine cold meat lunch, WRNS in attendance everything free including cable home, address P.O. box 164 ECI. Went to RAF Transit Camp given lots of kit. Everything very expensive. Newspaper columns on Almanzora incident & SEAC commission. Evidently row has reached ears at Blighty. P.O.W.'s ashore with us from "Nieuw Holland". ENSA party aboard, didn't go to show; film show at 10 p.m., I went; fine patriotic film, felt like "joining up" again. Were also given "spam' medal while ashore.

September 25, 1945, Tuesday

Bought 15 jewel gold watch for 12 today. 9 a.m. up-anchored & steamed out of Colombo. Great send-off, sirens tooting, R.A.F. launch circling round, navy lining decks of cruiser, carrier & destroyer, & even opened the end of an LCG, 3 cheers given & answered. 2nd stage of voyage now, regulations aboard now stricter. Clocks retarded 90 mins tonight, 2 1/2 hrs since leaving Singapore.

September 26, 1945, Wednesday

Sea intensely blue today, forced to remark about it. Stiff breeze, rain about 4 p.m. 2 pm took part in Whist Dreive w/o's mess. 5.0 p.m. passed lighthouse off Southernmost tip of India. Making better speed now than on 1st stage of voyage, if the tubes hold!

September 27, 1945, Thursday

Yesterday we had first beer issue of voyage, one pint, plus ½ pint issue of minerals. 2p.m. bridge with Matron & Padre, 2000 points up. 4.30 p.m. boat-stations. 7.30-9 pm a dance was held on E portside, poorly attended by women; more a less a washout. Raining & blowing small gale at 9 pm.

September 28, 1945, Friday

Clocks retarded 1 hour during night. 3 ½ hrs altogether now. Yesterday, met lady on board who had lived many years on & off in Weymouth, born in J. and speaks fluent Japanese. Am promised introduction to a young lady from Cattistock, by Matron. Pay today £1, beer issue, 1 bottle & 1 bottle of ginger beer.

September 29, 1945, Saturday

Hope to pass Aden tomorrow, abrupt drop of temperature during morning. It is noticeable how few fellows drink their beer issue, indeed I couldn't give mine away! 3 ½ yrs abstinence or milk-bar influence. O.C. troops steadily making himself unpopular. Stopped free issue of cigs. Because of smoking below decks, but these are from Red Cross & therefore he's not entitled to stop them. He may yet have to answer to the English press about it, especially as "civvies" are concerned. 2 p.m. played bridge with Matron & Padre. Lost heavily. Quite cold on deck everyone wearing his shirt. 4 p.m. dance on deck, few attending. Formal occupation of Java by English troops, Indonesians don't want Netherlands back.

September 30, 1945, Sunday

A cold, rough, windy night. Had nasty fall from hammock due to ship's tossing, half sprained right foot and left wrist. Doctor froze bruise with ethyl-chloride. I learned today, that so great was our knowledge of Jap defenses, tunnels etc on Singapore that on Allied landing, we were to be executed! Fine afternoon blue tranquil sea, warm sun, now at a lower angle, passed an island of Sokotra group, with appearance of snow covered, probably white sand & bleak. School of porpoises provided distraction swimming under bow, leaping in & out of the water; roughly 6' long, pink snouts.

October 1, 1945, Monday

This is to be the great month, our arrival back home. A very warm night as we progress through the Red Sea. Clocks retarded 1 hr. 4 ½ in all now. Should reach Aden tonight. Sweltering heat all day, impossible to keep cool, wrote letters home to Marianne, Peggy & Mum. Played bridge in afternoon, read "Lorna Doone", & watched at night, phosphorescent torpedo-like traits of porpoises diving at side of ship.

October 2, 1945, Tuesday

Just as hot as yesterday, but slight drop in temp. during afternoon; sweat rash prevalent. Passed islands of "12 apostles" with appearance of pyramid-like formation. On one, was a fort, another a lighthouse which was destroyed by Italians early on in war, & hasn't yet been restored. Good speed now, passed several ships. Had 1st official medical exam. Said that should probably get 28 days then report sick after leave for beriberi treatment in hospital. O.C. troops today appears to have capitulated on question of cig. issue.

October 3, 1945, Wednesday

Hot night, bathed in sweat. Woke at 5 am, sea almost without ripple, rind of moon giving golden path across a silvery sea; watched daybreak. On port bow a County cruiser, H.M.S. Devonshire passed us. Going east. Bridge in afternoon; won. Shore lights visible.

October 4, 1945, Thursday

Perceptibly cooler this morning, stiff breeze. calm sea. Should dock tomorrow. Saw Lt. Col., S.M.O. about my "os calcis" or heel bone. Thinks it is o.k. Bridge 2 p.m., 4.30 pm "Boat Stations." Beautiful sunset, throwing land on starboard into bold relief.

October 5, 1945, Friday

Awoke to a cool morning stiff breeze, land on port & st"board, converging to Port Tewfik. Passed by P&O liner "Carthage" doing about 18 knots intent on racing us into port. 4 pm. Just about to anchor, hot looking, arid place, mountainous with red haze overhanging, a narrow bottle neck harbourage in appearance with sundry shipping. Anchored in bay about 4.15 p.m., entrance to Suez visible in distance & at night it was illuminated by a row of green lights with one red overhead. It was quite cold during night. Some mail aboard, had note from Ceylon Command about Reg's address, unknown there.

October 6, 1945, Saturday

At 7.30 am. We pulled alongside wharf on opposite side of harbor to Port Tewfik. A military band played outside, cranes were decorated with flags of all the Allies, a huge banner said "Welcome on your way home. From M.E.F. Bon Voyage" A diesel train waited on wharf to take 1st consignment of chaps right around bay to Tewfik to be kitted at Ordnance depots. This side of Suez bay is called Adabiya, & went there ashore, first going to "Sandy Beach" a service resort with Naafi wagons, tents & bathing. I came back then to a camp called "1001 Co." to a big Naafi, bought Peggy a swim-suit, leather writing case, 2 wallets, & all & sundry toilet gear, also purchased. 1.30 pm ashore again, entrained in diesel & went round bay to Ataka, where, in huge hangers, surrounded by desert, was a gaily beflagged Naafi with all food free, band playing, & another full of kit, where I received blue. Returned to ship at 5 pm. I met German prisoners of war, formerly of Rommel's "Afrika Korps". Tucher spoke in German to some, I spoke in English to others; they said they were decently treated & fed, no news for 18 months of wife & family, seemed decent chaps & rather respectful. Saw white camels & Camel Corps, also Bermuda troops. RAF band came aboard but didn't see it. Bought 2 ladies' handbags for £1 each over side of ship. Still in bay as I go to bed in our former anchorage.

October 7, 1945, Sunday

Sunrise over Suez; the sun rising behind far sandstone ridges of desert turned skyline to a coppery hue & a rippleless sea to a sandy red. On our s'board bow forward, is anchored an aircraft carrier of R.N. 7.30 a.m. entered Suez Canal, a beautiful sight. Trim buildings of white & pink stone & trimmed hedges around like old box hedges in West Country. Above these were stately date palms, all foliage being of an intensely bright green hue, contrasted strongly with the sandstone ridges in desert, with rising sun glinting on them. A road runs parallel with canal, tar-mac. Lined by conifers about 6' apart, 2.45 pm passed officer's club & men's club, many ribald remarks & good humoured quips exchanged. The aircraft carrier "Activity"precedes us all the way. The little official stations with signal yards outside, blockhouse type buildings, vivid emerald-green borders, conifers & palms are fine looking oasis in this expanse of drift sand. Tented camps are visible in places, bivouac tents in plenty, & occasional camel stables their occupants squatting outside. Arrived at magnificent Suez entrance at 6.10 pm earlier than expected. Town of Suez very modern in appearance, fine stone buildings, palm lined streets, swarms of bumboats, searchlights beaming down from steel pylons; we anchored behind aircraft carrier, not far from "de Lessep's" statue. This is Port Said proper, Port Fuad is opposite. 7.45 pm. Preceded by tugs, we nosed our way outwards and some minutes later were on our way into the Med.

October 8, 1945, Monday

Dawn on the Mediterranean Ocean, no longer a tropical dawn with a sun hurtling over the rim, but a stealthy dawn just as in old times in Blighty. Spent morning tailoring my blues (my girth has certainly increased) bridge with Matron at 2 p.m. I'm afraid that I didn't find this Med. any bluer than any other ocean; this evening I observed my first twilight for 4 ½ years, the sea then seemed a deep indigo, probably influenced by failing light. The 1st batch of Ex. POW's arrived back from Far East (Rangoon), only 1 RAF man (a Cpl.) was there and was greeted by senior officers of R.A.F. Clocks retarded 1 hour, 5 ½ hrs in all from Sing

October 9, 1945, Tuesday

The coldest night we have yet had; will soon be in blues I am sure. I was introduced to Sister Dean from Battistock this morning by Matron, & had my heel massaged afterwards. Quite cold all day changed into my Burma jungle outfit. Vaccination in afternoon, bridge afterwards. Weird mixture of uniforms, some jungle green, some khaki & some winter clothing. Clocks to be retarded again 6 ½ hours from sing.

October 10, 1945, Wednesday

Less cold today, slept below for 1st time, started to embroider props. Badge. Bridge in afternoon. 4 pm. Sicily sighted on Starboard & 5.15 p.m., passing Malta on port side.

October 11, 1945, Thursday

Awoke early, temperature mild, & at 7.30 a.m. were passing Cape Bond of Tunisia. This coast on the portside was visible & close all the day; to think that this is the land which saw the defeat of Rommel's forces! Cliffs are of stratified sandstone, & white edifices visible here & there. Weather continued mild; I spent most of day below finishing my props.

October 12, 1945, Friday

Clocks retarded 1 hour last night; we are now back to Blighty time! A nice warm sunny day, pleasanter than tropical heat, the sea vivid bluer, as the Med. should be, under a cloudless blue sky. Coastline visible on port bow all day. Passed sundry ships today including one Portuguese. Bridge in afternoon & a surprise "Boat stations."

October 13, 1945, Saturday

Vaccination "taken," some irritation. Weather on deck mild & sunny. From 1 pm onwards the coastline of Spain was visible, rugged & mountainous. At 2 pm. A boxing tournament was held, the Captain giving prizes of cigarettes away. 5 pm. Just passing the rock of Gibraltar with African coastline visible to port. Clouds hanging over the grim rock face give the appearance of a mushroom top, and the temperature drops rapidly as the sun sets behind the mountains of Portugal. 5.15 pm anchored in bay; houses have the appearance of being many storied, white cliffs rise sheer from sea, & on top lonely A.A. & searchlight batteries appear so solitary that defenders have name of "Gibraltar Monkeys." Night in the bay, a sickle moon rising off the African coast, a myriad lights twinkling on shore, but not clustered together as in most towns, but scattered afar &

rising above each other since the buildings are grouped in terraces. Bright lights of motorboats & other vessels illuminate the western (Spanish) side of the bay.

October 14, 1945, Sunday

Dawn on the Atlantic, on the fourth & final stage of our voyage, with a sea already blue. green in its colour & a cloudy sky. We must have left in the vicinity of midnight, while I slept, after oiling & watering, & now we shan't be long. At 8 a.m. a battleship was visible on the horizon to port. The temperature was mild, & we still on tropical wear. 1.30 p.m. we rounded the Cape, the cliffs of which rise perpendicular, of a pleasing sandstone appearance, but strangely enough the cliff top is flat & level, giving the impression of an ideal spot for an aerodrome. On the point itself is a white building with a lighthouse attached. To which we signaled with the siren on passing it. Now, as the lads say, we "turn right" or starboard the helm for home & beauty At 8 p.m. on the starboard bow a cluster of lights were discernible, some Portuguese town evidently.

October 15, 1945, Monday

Cool on deck, with a green-blue sea, but not at all rough; still in tropical kit, even if it is drizzly. Later on weather cleared, grew perceptibly colder & the sea to a greyish blue. 3 p.m. we passed Cape Finisterre, not closely enough for clear vision. During the afternoon an impromptu exhibition of

water-colour paintings of P.O.W. life on the Burma-Siam
cholera camps & general P.O.W. life in Changi jail was
given by a soldier Charles Thrale of Caterham Surrey who
intends to have books made by photo-engraver. I donned
blues for the first time, in the evening; apart from the smart
feeling of dressing up, was aware of an unpleasant restricted
& "bottled-up" feeling. At 7.0 pm there was a crazy night
show in W.O.'s lounge with all sorts of entertainments.

October 16, 1945, Tuesday

Awoke in the morning in middle of Bay of Biscay the hammock riding up & down with the ship's motion. Sea had a
fair swell, but not unduly rough, a cerulean sea, misty sun,
& the aft end of the ship heaving out of, & burying itself
in, the foam. Two thirds of the mess went without breakfast
& were stretched out like so many corpses. On F weather
deck, there was a real sting in the wind, a fine invigorating
spray with the breeze. Spent most of the day on deck until
5 pm we passed through the cyclone belt to a calmer sea
& watery sun. Later in the evening with a fair swell and a
rising moon it was really bracing. Last packing completed
tonight & all set for the great day ahead.

October 17, 1945, Wednesday

Awoke early for the great move. A cold morning dull sea &
no land in sight. All kitbags and hammocks had to be carried up to D starboard deck for stacking & the keen wind

just whistled through one while climbing the iron companionways. 10 a.m. sighted Channel Is. Off starboard bow in distance. 11 am we were off Poole & coast of England just visible at 11.40 a.m. At 12.45 I.O.W. on starboard & Bournemouth on port; passed Needles 12.45 pm. 1 p.m. passed Freshwater & Colwell & on the port Hurst castle. 7.15 we docked in Southampton after a wonderful reception by everyone. Just before arrival I received 7 letters 4 from Mum, 2 from Peggy. & 1 from G.P.O. B'mouth. A fine speech was made to us & a message from King & Queen read to us. On the quayside was a reception committee of High officers, nurses & the RAF band. The violent hooting of all the tugs in the harbor affected us most of all, & we all felt choky in the throat. The RAF went straight ashore to a waiting train in shed. I spoke to a nice old Air Commodore there. 4.30. p.m. we left there' in special express, stopping at Basingstoke at 6.0 pm & had refreshments from WAAFS from Andover, then a second stop at Banbury at 9.0 p.m. At 9.45 pm reached Birmingham & 1015 p.m. Cosford station. Received by a Group Capn & taken to camp in lorries, straight into hanger to report & give particulars & 11.15 a dinner of fish & peas. Went to hut P11, new address 106 P.R.C.

October 18, 1945, Thursday

Awoke at 6 a.m. washed and dressed. Huts are of some standard pattern as in old days. I felt rather like joining up again. 7.30 a.m. breakfast. 8.30 a.m. went to 106 P.R.C. & obtained kit, £19 pay, £2 ration money included, initial payment of £398 in P.O., medical examination by a Sq. Ldr. Who seemed to know his gen on tropical diseases. Was promoted to Corporal today, some fellows jumped from LAC to FL/SGT. Some even became officers, one a FL. LT. Had tapes sewn on, tons of joking, received travelling warrant & ration cards. Bought 6 weeks supply of chocolate and cigarettes, & by 4.0 pm was all ready to go home. London fellows left at 4.15 p.m. but I & others from south leave at 9.53 am tomorrow.

October 19, 1945, Friday

Awoke early at 6 am ready for "Der Tag". 7.30 am breakfast & saw first batch off at 8 am & left to catch 9.53 am train from Cosford. Reached Shrewsbury & changed to train through Wales to Bristol via Severn tunnel. RTO were warned all the way down by phone & were waiting & helped me with my kit. At Bristol waited for 5.3 pm train & sent phone call via RTO to Broadwey P.O. to warn everyone in advance. Chatted to people in train & helped to amuse a couple of curly-headed babies. Reached UPWEY Junc. at 8.30 pm. to see dear old Mum, Aunty & Mr. Rogers waiting for me. Went home in car to house bedecked gaily with flags & neighbors all waiting as reception committee for me. Lots to talk about, inevitable speech on every topic imaginable a dainty spread to delight the eye of any x POW

& above all to find that little has altered since I left; and by the merciful providence of the Almighty I have reached my journey's end & thy "place where I would be" and thus closes another chapter of my life with all its pains & sorrows, but leading to a great "Renaissance" & a life which I trust with God's help will not be void of love of those most dear to me nor the faith of past & present friends.

Thus ends the diary of my journey back to life.

THE END

EPILOGUE

My dad returned to England and his loving family. He met up with Peggy on bicycles one day. After brief greetings, she spoke to him of going away to college. Without further emotion, she merely rode out of sight. He never saw her again. In April 1947, he married his fiancé, Mary Patricia Mason. The two honeymooned on the Island of Jersey in the English Channel. My parents left England and emigrated to Canada and then the United States. They lived in New Hampshire, Vermont, North Carolina, New Jersey, and finally, Newtown, Connecticut. Dad became an ordained Catholic Deacon and served the Diocese of Bridgeport, Connecticut, from 1978 to 2000. He is now Deacon Emeritus, the oldest deacon and the longest ordained in the Diocese of Bridgeport. He and Mom became US citizens. He was previously a communications engineer and had worked for ITT for twenty-five years until his retirement in 1985. His work in telecommunications in Europe and Africa was the foundation of the Internet. On one trip to Beirut, Lebanon, in the 1970s, Dad was working at a satellite earth station antenna on a large hilltop. He traveled into the city one day with a fellow engineer driving the car. A civil unrest was occurring in Lebanon at the time. As they entered an intersection, they were fired upon. The engineer driving, completely traumatized, pulled over, and began to light up a cigarette. Dad yelled at him, "Let's get out of here!" He readily complied. Dad escaped death yet again.

On November 14, 1977, Dad attended a lecture at his office building in Stamford, Connecticut. The lecture was being given by a brilliant engineer from England, Ivor Catt. Intrigued by his last name, Dad approached Catt and told him that the only other Catt he ever met, Syd Catt, was during the war in Singapore. The engineer, astounded, told Dad that Syd Catt was his father! Dad told Ivor that he assumed Syd had been executed when the Japs marched him out of the camp one day. Ivor told him that not only did Syd survive, but he lived happily in Kent, England. Dad told Ivor that the night he had dinner at Syd's house in Singapore, he never met Syd's children. Ivor replied that he and his sister had been upstairs asleep that night when my dad was there visiting.

In 1978, I made a trip to England with my mom and dad. We drove down a long, winding country lane in Kent to the home of Syd Catt and his wife, Enid. I finally got to meet the man who had been so good to my father, and I thanked him for it. Over copious cups of tea, Syd told us his fascinating story. He had been taken to Japan where he was eventually interrogated. When he was grilled about ciphers, he acted in a bizarre fashion, and the Jap brass wrote him off as crazy. He survived. He even showed me a Rolex watch he had that had been given to him by an American flyer during the war. What a fascinating man. I was humbled by him. Sydney E. Catt died in November 1986.

The dropping of the atomic bomb saved my father's life and the lives of thousands of other Allied prisoners of war. If the mainland of Japan had been invaded, the Japanese High Command circulated orders that *all* POWs were to be executed. The prisoners would have stood as evidence of the atrocities that the Japanese had committed. *Quod Erat Demonstrandum.* As it was, many thousands were indeed executed and dumped into common graves on desert islands.

My father is not bitter about the war. He holds no malice in his heart for the Japanese. Once, while walking down a hall at work, he came upon a group of engineering visitors. They were from Japan. A woman leading them was obviously an interpreter. My father, intrigued, stopped and said a few words to her in Japanese. The woman, quite impressed, asked Dad how he knew the language. Dad simply replied, "I was in a Japanese prisoner of war camp in World War II."

The Japanese woman, visibly ashamed, bowed to him and said, "Let me apologize." In the mid-1990s, my mother and father received a small amount of money that was sent to them by the British Government. The money was from Japanese assets that the British had liquidated and turned back to the former POWs. In my opinion, the entire Mitsubishi Corporation should have been liquidated and paid to these men! In her book *Unjust Enrichment*, author Linda Goetz Holmes states, "Altogether about 25,000 American POWs found themselves doing slave labor at Japanese factories, shipyards and mines including at major companies such as Mitsui and Nippon. More than 40 Japanese companies used prisoners under these conditions." Mom and Dad used the money to take a trip to the Holy Land together and turned a negative experience into a wonderful, spiritual one.

My uncle Reg told me once what it was like to fight the Japs in Burma. He said that Jap snipers would lash themselves onto the limb of a tree high up. They would wait all day to finally shoot a British officer passing underneath. When this occurred, Reg and the others circled the tree and poured Sten gun fire into the sniper, blasting him in to bits. They searched many Japanese soldiers that they encountered and killed. These soldiers had on them a fish head and a ball of rice. They could subsist on this for days!

What a tenacious enemy. Uncle Reg once said to me very seriously, "The dropping of the bomb saved my life. I was slated to be in the invading force that would land on the Japanese shore."

The Japanese guards who carried out atrocities in Java were brought to justice. Some met their demise at the end of American or British ropes. Others rotted in prison. Lord Louis Mountbatten, when he visited dad's camp, made certain that his men collected the names of the guards that had abused my dad and the other men. He followed up with swift British justice.

History has judged the surrender of the Allied forces in Singapore with great disdain. In my opinion, England suffered two sad chapters in its history; the evacuation from Dunkirk and the fall and subsequent surrender of Singapore. I can only feel bitter that my dad and men like him were not lead by better men who should have looked out for them. To have men in a combat zone, without arms, is reprehensible. When I think about England, with great pride, I think about its military's history. Waterloo, Roark's Drift, and many other battles exemplify the British fighting spirit. We have seen the magnificence of the SAS commandos in recent wars. But Singapore was a disaster. It should never have happened. The leaders in that area at that time should have been better men. They should have had a plan. The equipment that the British had was inadequate. Their training had not prepared them for what lay ahead. Much the same can be said about the Americans at Corregidor. Admittedly, I was a cop and not a soldier. In my occupation, we could never surrender, and we had to win every engagement. But I did learn in my long career that you must wisely pick your battles and realize that some things are not worth dying for.

I had a wonderful childhood in the 1960s, with many fond memories of my dad. We lived in Raleigh, North Carolina, at the time. My world was filled with school and watching TV shows about World War II. I looked up to my father and was proud of him, and especially proud of his service in the war and his and my mom's long family service in both World War I and World War II. My family was very religious, pro-government, and pro-law enforcement. I was so inspired by stories that my dad told me about his police officer father, that from the time I was five I knew I would become a police officer also. My career as a cop exposed me to all the violence and death that one could imagine. I would often call my dad after a gruesome scene and share the details with him. The worst calls were the ones involving the death of children. I knew he, more than most people, would understand. I saw what bullets could do to the human body, and I gained a very great respect for what soldiers in combat must endure.

I remember one night; I was on patrol in my cruiser. I pulled over a car after the driver drove through a red light. I approached the driver's side of the car and saw immediately that the occupants were an older couple. I asked the driver for his paperwork, and he was visibly shaking. He and his wife's eyes looked from my hat, to my uniform, and down to the gun in my holster. They appeared absolutely frightened to death. As he handed me his license, his shirt sleeve exposed his forearm. I saw a series of faded numbers tattooed on his arm. He spoke with a heavy accent. My throat tightened. I said to him, "Auschwitz?" He nodded sadly and said "yes." I handed him back his paperwork and said, "Have a nice evening." As I walked back to my car, I was choked with emotion. I had met another like my dad who had suffered so much. I have asked my dad many times what each day was like. My children were curious as to what each day smelled like, felt like. He told me he kept a constant faith in God and this sustained him and gave him hope. The days were long and blended into months and then years. Men died and had to be buried. Disease, dysentery, and despair were constant problems. The excessive heat baked the men's bodies constantly. They only bathed by jumping into the river while under guard. He told me that he would wake up each morning and wonder if he would be one of those who would make it. He wondered where it was all leading them. It is unimaginable to think that he and all those other men were in their early twenties. Their whole lives were ahead of them.

The lack of food and their empty bellies were paramount in their daily thoughts. As children, my family was rigidly taught to never waste food. We always tried to clean our plates and finish, and appreciate, every meal. When dad would pour us drinks at dinner, he always placed two fingers against the side of the glass. As a father, I could not help myself from issuing my children the requisite two finger liquid portions as well, even to this day, when my children are now adults. Dad once observed native people pulling grass strands from the ground. They showed him what parts of the grass were edible and he ate it, gratefully. Once over dinner at my home many years ago, my wonderful neighbors Bob and Irene Wiegers brought Bob's parents over. They were marvelous and fascinating people. My mom and dad were also there. Astoundingly, after a brief discussion, my dad realized that Bob's parents had grown up on one of the islands he had been held prisoner on! Bob's mom, as a very young girl, remembered seeing Allied POWs march past her town. Dad's life has been a collection of many miraculous coincidences.

My father is a proud man. He is proud of England, and he was proud to be in the Royal Air Force. When France fell, these brave airmen stood their ground in a legendary air war with the Luftwaffe. Thank God they persevered. I quote here the famous words of Winston Churchill: "The gratitude of every home in our Island, in our Empire, and indeed throughout the world, except in the abodes of the guilty, goes out to the British airmen who, undaunted by odds, unwearied in their constant challenge and mortal danger, are turning the tide of the World War by their prowess and by their devotion. *Never in the field of human conflict was so much owed by so many to so few*".

The bravery that all the POWs of World War II showed, and the suffering that they endured, will never be forgotten. I am grateful for such men whose brave acts have allowed me a life that I now enjoy. May God watch over these men, and may he give rest to those who lie in graves unknown in those islands. Pax Britannica.